Longshaw
in the Peak District
DERBYSHIRE

A souvenir guide

 THE NATIONAL TRUST

THE SECRETS OF LONGSHAW

For 8,000 years, people have lived and worked in the rugged landscape of Longshaw – farming, trading, hunting and quarrying.

Why Longshaw?
The first-known reference to 'Longshaw' was in 1722. 'Shaw' is an old term for small wood or copse, and so presumably Longshaw means 'long wood' – which may be a reference to Padley Gorge.

Above A beech tree grows amongst the rocks of Padley Gorge

Stepping back in time

Criss-crossed by old trackways and packhorse trails, Longshaw was once at the crossroads of important trading routes for salt, silk, cotton, wool, coal and lead. Its own wealth of natural resources also made it an important place for early industry.

It may be difficult to imagine now, but just a few hundred years ago parts of Longshaw were busy with the noise of charcoal burning and gritstone quarrying. The oak woods provided the fuel for local lead smelting; and the coarse stone was carved to form millstones. Much of the evidence of this early industrial activity still lies abandoned in the woods all around Longshaw.

The eerie atmosphere of Bole Hill, cloaked in silver birch, conceals the old quarry workings – now silent – of an industry that provided over one million tons of stone for the nearby Derwent and Howden dams further up the Derwent Valley.

The woods and moors were once the favourite haunt of shooting parties who stayed at the Duke of Rutland's hunting retreat at Longshaw Lodge. Signs of the Duke's influence can still be seen around Longshaw. Look out for the white gates as you take a walk around.

Wildlife haven

Longshaw is a haven for rare woodland wildlife. Huge dome-shaped nests built by hairy wood ants can be seen in the shady woods. Pied flycatchers fly in each spring from Africa to rear their young in the ancient oak trees, and unusual mosses and ferns cling to the rocky waterfalls and springs.

Rare species of fungi thrive in the grasslands, and each summer the haymeadows are awash with wildflowers, providing food to a host of buzzing insects.

On higher ground, moorland birds nest amongst the heather, which fills the air with its honey-scented bloom in late summer.

Today and tomorrow

Today, sheep and cattle graze the meadows long since cleared of trees. And future generations will discover new stories about this place, as the landscape responds to changes in the way it is managed.

Above left An outcrop of millstone grit on Longshaw's tranquil moorland

Below A nuthatch

LANDSCAPE AND WILDLIFE

MEADOWS, GRASSLAND AND MOORLAND

The Longshaw Estate stretches from the high windswept moorlands of Burbage and White Edge down to the quiet waters of the River Derwent in the valley below, and its rich mixture of grassland habitats varies with the changes in the landscape.

Above Millstone grit and heather moorland

Left Field scabious

Longshaw has benefited from a long period of low-impact farming, where few chemical fertilisers, and only small amounts of animal manure have been used. This careful management has produced the wide variety of grasses, flowers and other plants you can see today.

The moorland parts of Longshaw, including Lawrence Field and White Edge, have seen a big increase in the heathland plants recently. There are fewer sheep grazing, so the heather has flourished, which is perfect for insects and ground-nesting birds like the red grouse.

Steeper and rougher areas of grassland like Square Field in Haywood have never been fertilised for farming, and so rare and exciting plants, including twayblade orchids and adders tongue fern, can be found growing there.

In the flatter haymeadow fields below the Grouse Inn you can now find yellow rattle, pignut, meadow vetch, field scabious, black knapweed, oxeye daisy and common spotted orchids. (If you go for a walk around here, please keep to the footpaths to avoid damaging the valuable hay crop.)

The cry of the curlew

On some of the wetter fields near the moorland edge, rushes grow in large areas. These are cut by tractor at the end of the summer to make ideal nesting grounds for curlew and other wading birds in the springtime. Listen out for the haunting cry of the curlew as it flies over the moors.

WOODLAND MAGIC

The ancient oaks of Yarncliff and Padley Woods, gnarled and twisting out of gritstone rocks, are survivors of the oak-birch woodland that once covered much of the edges of the Peak District's gritstone uplands. Amongst the trees and rocks you can discover a whole host of plants and wildlife. Lichens, mosses and liverworts creep across gritstone boulders and abandoned, unfinished millstones. Pied flycatcher, nuthatch and hawfinch nest amongst the leafy branches each spring, whilst rover beetle and uncommon beetle burrow into decaying wood at your feet.

Padley Gorge is a tranquil place, where the sound of the wind in the trees combines with the birdsong and the splashing of Burbage Brook as it carves its way through the rocks from the high moors to join the River Derwent below. Oak, birch and rowan all thrive here, with alder alongside the brook and in damp hollows.

Other, quieter areas of woodland worth exploring are the open glades of Froggatt Wood, hidden amongst the oak and birch, which are home to redstarts, wood warblers and treecreepers.

Perhaps you could visit Bolehill Quarry Wood, a younger woodland with its birch-terraced floor, sheep-grazed grasses and hairy wood ant nests.

OPPOSITE

Left Oxhay Wood

Right Burbage Brook flows through Padley Woods

Below A female pied flycatcher

Why not see if you can spot a green woodpecker in Oxhay Wood?

FUNGAL DELIGHTS

Longshaw is an excellent place for fungi – both in the woods and on the open grasslands.

Longshaw's open grasslands are some of the richest in Britain for fungi, particularly *waxcaps*, of which more than 35 varieties have been recorded. Waxcaps are usually easy to spot. You can find them in all sorts of beautiful colours and they have a cap that is greasy to the touch. There are lots of different types of waxcap at Longshaw because many of its grassland areas have never been treated with artificial fertilisers and have a long history of traditional grazing. The mushroom or toadstool that we see is really just the tip of the growing fungus – like an apple growing on an apple tree. The vast bulk of it is made up of tiny, usually unseen filaments called the *mycelium* that spread through soil, rotting wood or other material.

The best time of year to search for fungi is autumn, though you can find them at other times too. Why not join one of the National Trust's fungi events that are held at Longshaw in autumn?

Left Scarlet waxcap (*Hygrocybe miniata*)

OPPOSITE
Left Meadow waxcap (*Hygrocybe pratensis*)
Right Golden waxcap (*Hygrocybe chlorophana*)

Fascinating fungi facts

Fungi are known as 'nature's recyclers' because they speed up the decay of dead plants and animals by using their nutrients for growth. Without them, we would all be buried under a pile of dead plants.

In the woods, look for branch- or club-shaped fungi. These fungi often grow with trees like birch and oak – linked to their root systems. Many are good at collecting nutrients and seem to 'swap' them for food from the tree.

Some fungi are edible, but others, like this fly agaric (pictured left), are deadly poisonous. Make sure you get expert advice on identification before eating them.

Did you know?

Fungi are neither plants nor animals, but form a kingdom of their own.

AMAZING ANTS

Huge numbers of the rare northern hairy wood ant can be found at Longshaw. These are large reddish ants which can build their nests up to 40 cm high. Look out for them in the woods or open grassland, especially near Scots pine trees.

Northern hairy wood ants are so called because they have hairy faces – but you'd have to look through a microscope to see them!

The ants are careful and expert builders of nests. They build a weatherproof roof of thatch to protect their tunnels from rain, frost and wind. Specialist workers are at the ready to carry out repairs to the thatch and they're also on hand to open up the tunnels for ventilation in hot weather or close the holes if it's cold or wet.

Each nest is carefully located to catch the warmth of the sun, which helps the ants' eggs and larvae to develop successfully. Sometimes in spring, the ants warm themselves in the sun at the surface and then 'carry' the warmth down into the nest.

Each nest can have several queens that produce tens of thousands of worker ants – possibly more than 250,000 per nest! Watch out for the ant trails that lead from the nest outwards into the surrounding habitat – but don't stand on them for too long!

Wood ants eat all sorts of other grubs and insects, but especially feed on the honey dew produced by aphids: have a look in the branches.

Left A northern hairy wood ant nest

Opposite

Top A northern hairy wood ant

Bottom Each nest can contain over a quarter of a million ants

Why not?

Listen On a warm and sunny day you can often hear the ants at work – get close to a nest and listen for the rustling sound.

Smell Northern hairy wood ants don't bite or sting, but they can spray formic acid from the tip of their abdomen. This acid is used for attack and defence, and sometimes for killing grasses that grow in front of the nest and block out the light. A whiff of the acid might remind you of salt and vinegar crisps!

Take care Northern hairy wood ants are rare in Europe – so please don't disturb their nests.

11

LOOKING AFTER LONGSHAW

SHAPING THE LANDSCAPE

People have lived on and shaped the Longshaw landscape for thousands of years, from the early settlers who built longhouses and farmed the land, to the visitors of today who come to enjoy the woods and moors.

People have always worked on the estate, making the most of the natural resources that Longshaw has to offer. The landscape that we see today has been managed for centuries. The National Trust continues to manage the Longshaw Estate in order to provide the fullest possible access for anyone who wants to enjoy the fantastic scenery, in balance with the needs of the people who live and work here. We also work continuously to protect forever the special habitats and wildlife of this living, working and ever-changing landscape.

There is a wide range of habitats to look after at Longshaw. Sheep and cattle can often be seen grazing the grasslands on the estate. Where they graze and for how long is carefully arranged with the farmers so that habitats for wildlife can be allowed to develop. Too much grazing, and plants will be lost, as they no longer get the chance to seed. Too little, and flowers will be choked by dense grasses.

Volunteers

The National Trust is a large organisation, but, being an independent charity, the number of full-time staff it employs is relatively small. The Trust has traditionally been supported in all aspects of its work by volunteers.

At Longshaw there has been a long tradition of volunteer working groups, helping the wardens with vital conservation work. The Clarion Ramblers have been volunteering at Longshaw since it was acquired by the Trust in 1931. The Mudlarks have been adding their support since the 1990s.

There are also a number of long-term volunteers, who have become part of the fabric of the estate. Their working knowledge of Longshaw and the time they have contributed to the estate continues to be invaluable.

12

Above A volunteer drystone-walling

Below Reed-clearing on a working holiday

A YEAR IN THE LIFE OF A LONGSHAW WARDEN

January

Woodland work, thinning trees and removing dangerous trees, drainage work on footpaths.

February

Lay hedges, prune trees near footpaths, repair drystone walls and fences ready for lambing time.

March

Put up nestboxes, do repairs to roadside walls after snow and ice, install new gates for easier access for visitors.

April

Organise Easter trails, put up signs about lambing. Unblock nestboxes ready for pied flycatchers to return. (Boxes were blocked to stop other birds nesting.)

May

Repair tracks and pathways after winter rain. Organise the annual Countryside Open Day event.

June

Support students on work experience, map bracken areas for spraying at the end of August, cut bracken on flat areas.

July

Monitor hay meadows, collect litter, stock up leaflet boxes, ready for the holiday season.

August

Organise working holiday groups, cut rushes on rough fields to encourage waders to nest in the spring, clear pond sedges, spray bracken.

September

Lay hedges, clear out drains and ditches ready for winter.

October

Tree inspections, looking for any unsafe trees which need work and attention. Monitor fungi in meadows.

November

Woodland work, thinning out plantations to allow room for the best trees to grow.

December

Christmas tree sales. Tree inspections and removing hazardous trees and branches.

HISTORY

ANCIENT TRACES

Below A guidestoop or waymarker, which guided travellers on the moors

Early settlements

The grassy mounds on Lawrence Field could be the remains of a settlement where the land was cleared of trees to form farmland. Within a large oval-shaped space are the remains of two longhouses. The smaller one was possibly used as an outhouse and is now overgrown with grass and heather. The larger building is easier to find – to the left of the path as it enters the trees. Pottery fragments have also been found here which have been dated to the 11th or 12th centuries, suggesting this is a late Saxon or early medieval settlement.

Packhorse trails

Packhorse trails criss-cross the Longshaw Estate. They are part of the industrial past of the area, when packhorse trains carried silk, cotton, lead and salt across the hills and valleys of the Peak District to the growing industrial centres of Manchester and Sheffield. Travelling across the moors took several days and could be treacherous, particularly if the weather turned foul and the mist descended. The Wooden Pole served as a guide on one of the old packhorse routes and marks the boundary between Hathersage and Holmesfield.

Do you recognise the names of local towns and villages which were carved onto this guidestoop in 1709?

SHAFILD
CHASTERFILD
TIDSWEL
HATHASICH and so to CHAPIL IN LEE FRITH

Below A medieval packhorse from the Luttrell Psalter

Guidestoops

The two guidestoops you can find still standing on the Longshaw Estate are remnants of a time when travellers could easily lose their way on the moors. The Scandinavian word 'stoop' means stone. There is also a 1758 milepost standing in Longshaw Meadow, on the site of the old turnpike from Sheffield to Buxton, before the road was moved to its current position in the 1830s.

Left The ancient trackway of Hollowgate, near Burbage Brook. Here the heather clings to the banks on either side of the sunken track, worn away by hundreds of years of use

NORTHERN GRIT

The earliest known records of millstone-making at Longshaw date back to 1466, when Ralph and Robert Eyre, who lived at Padley Hall, employed two millstone-makers, one of whom was called Jankyn Stonhewer.

Making millstones was hard work. The millstone grit was quarried out of the ground and then the stone cutters worked by hand, using chisels and hammers for days at a time to create the perfectly circular stones. The stones were measured in hands and could be as much as 15 or 16 hands in diameter (nearly 1.5 metres across). They were usually sold in pairs. Stones were bought for three reasons: to grind grain for flour; to pulp timber to make paper; and for use as grindstones to sharpen blades in the Sheffield steel industry.

Each of these industries saw times of prosperity and decline, and the demand for stones fluctuated with them. Peak District millstones began to fall out of favour, as the desire for finer and whiter flour resulted in more effective stones being imported from France and Germany during the 16th century.

Grindstones made from millstone grit could be dangerous. When the stones were turning at high speeds, any flaws could make them explode, causing injury or even death. A cheaper and safer compound of carbon and silicon known as 'carborundum' was invented in America, so the need for millstone grit declined.

Below and opposite Abandoned grindstones at the entrance to Bolehill Quarry

Why not see if you can find some of the many abandoned stones at Longshaw, gathering lichens and mosses in Bole Hill Wood and at the top of Padley Gorge? The stacked grindstones below Surprise View were removed from Bole Hill Quarry when work began on quarrying stone for the Derwent dams.

WHO BUILT LONGSHAW LODGE AND WHY?

The Lodge was built by the 5th Duke of Rutland as his 'shooting box' close to the moors where he often enjoyed grouse shooting.

The Duke and his shooting parties could return to the comfort of the lodge after days hunting grouse on the moors. It was always relatively luxurious, with ornamental gardens and an ice-house supplied with ice from the newly dug pond. There was also a series of private walks and drives created through the estate, and a plunge pool where guests could cool off on hot summer days. The many rhododendrons near the lodge were planted to provide cover for game and continue to flower every summer. The Duke's influence on Longshaw lasted for just over 100 years. The old ice-house remains behind the lodge, now dark and empty, and you can also still find many of the original white ducal gates at old driveway entrances around the estate.

The Duke owned extensive areas of moorland from Ringinglow to Robin Hood near Baslow. The present Longshaw Estate is just a tiny fragment of this. We don't know exactly when the Lodge was built, but probably around 1827. The Duke also constructed another nine smaller lodges around the estate to house his gamekeepers. One of these is White Edge Lodge, which is now a National Trust holiday cottage (see p.28).

Above John Henry Manners, 5th Duke of Rutland, who built Longshaw Lodge. He was said at his death in 1857 to have been 'of a tall and noble presence, exceedingly elegant and dignified in manner, but was singularly courteous in his reception of those who had business with him'

The famous **Longshaw sheep-dog trials** are reputed to have started as a competition between the Duke's head shepherd and head gamekeeper in 1898 – and have continued ever since in early September on the meadow in front of the lodge. They claim to be the oldest sheep-dog trials in the country.

BLOOD OUT OF STONE

In the early 1900s the cities of Sheffield, Nottingham, Derby and Leicester were rapidly expanding and needed a water supply to match. Where was the water to come from? The nearby moors of the Peak District provided the answer.

In 1901 the Derwent Valley Water Board decided to build two dams to create the reservoirs which would store and supply water to the growing industrial centres. Thousands of tons of millstone grit would be needed to build these two enormous dams.

Before the huge task of quarrying the stone out of Bolehill Quarry could begin, transport had to be arranged, both within and from the quarry at Padley. Railway tracks were laid through the woods, including a cable line down a steep incline to carry the dressed stone

Dambusting

The dams at the Derwent and Howden reservoirs were the training ground for the bouncing bombs used in the famous Dambusters raid of World War II, and feature in the Dambusters film.

to Grindleford station. From there the rock was transported through Bamford and up to the Derwent Valley. Production at Bolehill continued until December 1910. The Derwent Valley Water Board gave the quarry to the National Trust in 1947.

Exploring Bolehill

You can now enjoy a peaceful woodland walk along the broad, grassy tracks which were once busy with the noise of the railway.

At the top of the incline in amongst the birch trees you will find the remains of the building that housed the big winding drum. From this drum, cables ran down the incline to the railway line below. The cables helped to keep the carriages on track as the weight of a fully loaded carriage going down the steep slope would pull the empty ones back up to the top.

Accidents and injuries

Work at the quarry was dangerous, and there were many accidents, resulting in serious injury or death. Dr Lander of Hathersage came to the aid of many injured quarrymen, but sadly was not always able to save them.

12 February 1903

William Brewster, aged 29 from Hathersage, was working at the foot of the inclined railway when three carriages broke loose and came hurtling down the steep slope towards him. William died almost immediately from 'shock to his system, a compound leg fracture and ruptured intestines'.

Opposite The Derwent Valley reservoir still supplies water to Sheffield and other nearby cities

On the same day, but working at the quarry face the elderly John Schofield, also from Hathersage, and Christopher Youle from Bamford were steadying a huge stone hanging from a crane when the couplers slipped and they were both flung ten feet to the foot of the quarry. John suffered a cut to his head and crushed ribs, but Christopher luckily managed to get away with only minor injuries.

By 1903 the best workmen had received a pay rise of 1 penny and could earn up to 8 1/2d per hour (around 4p). This was quite a good wage at the time, equivalent today to around £3 per hour.

Left A railway line was constructed to carry stone from the quarry to the sites of the dams

REST AND RECUPERATION AT LONGSHAW

Longshaw was used as a hospital for injured soldiers during the First World War.

The Military Base Hospital in Sheffield was overflowing with sick and wounded soldiers brought to England from the front line. In February 1915 the Duke of Rutland offered the use of his lodge as a base for convalescing patients, and Longshaw became a 'Base Hospital Section', along with many schools and other smaller district hospitals, which looked after injured soldiers for the rest of the war.

Opposite Neil Kenyon
Below Sergeant Charles Richards, Royal Welch Fusiliers, September 1915

An album of memories

Mrs Alice Clifford used to visit the soldiers at Longshaw, and arranged recreational activities and entertainment for them. She also kept an album of photographs, autographs and other details of life at Longshaw during the war. Alice was the wife of Charles Clifford, Managing Director of the *Sheffield Daily Telegraph*.

Longshawe Lodge Hospital Summer 1915. Derbyshire

'In the wards a number of the most recently arrived soldiers were resting. One and all seemed full of quiet content and very happy in their new home. This feeling was voiced by an Irishman, who, looking up and seeing several snowflakes fall, said he wished they might be snowed in, then they would not have to go.'

Sheffield Daily Telegraph, **27 February 1915**

Revelations

Many young women from middle- and upper-class homes offered their services as VADs (Voluntary Aid Detachments) to assist the medical services. Nothing in their previously sheltered lives could have prepared them for the conditions in which they later lived and worked. The soldiers' language was shocking, and some women admitted to having only a vague notion of what a man looked like with no clothes on before the war. In *Testament of Youth*, Vera Brittain wrote, 'Short of actually going to bed with them, there was hardly an intimate service that I did not perform for one or another in the course of four years'.

A sad story: Cyril Charles Newbury

The Newbury family had emigrated from the Channel Islands to New Zealand in 1874 where they opened a baker's shop in Dunedin, Otago. Cyril Newbury joined up in January 1915 aged 21. His medical examination records him being 5ft 8in tall, weighing 9st 12lbs, with a fair complexion and flaxen hair.

However, Cyril's army career was sadly short-lived. After training, he set sail for Alexandria in Egypt in April 1915, then left to join his unit at Anzac Cove in June. Less than a month later, he was in a Greek hospital suffering from diarrhoea, sent to a hospital ship and then on to Malta, where he was diagnosed with dysentery. By the end of the month he was suffering from shellshock.

In September Cyril was transferred to Sheffield and was sent to convalesce at Longshaw, where he was described as 'slightly sick, progressing well'. Hopefully, he was able to make the most of his beautiful surroundings before being deemed fit for active service. He left Longshaw in March 1916 to rejoin his unit and by April had embarked for the front line in France.

Sadly, just three months later, Cyril was killed in action at Armentières and was buried in the Cité Bonjean military cemetery.

Above left A wartime winter at Longshaw Lodge

OPPOSITE

Top Cyril Newbury (standing, in uniform) with his family
Below left Alice Clifford kept the report of Cyril Newbury's death in her album

Private Cyril C. Newbury, of the Otago Regiment, New Zealand Forces, was killed in France on the 8th inst, by shrapnel whilst standing near his dug-out. He was wounded in the Dardanelles campaign of last year, and invalided to Sheffield Base Hospital, afterwards to Longshaw Lodge, Grindleford. His death will be greatly regretted by the many friends he made when in Sheffield. Captain Louis G. Wilson, in charge of his company, writes thanking Sheffield friends for their hospitality so readily extended to Private Newbury whilst in the city.

July 1916.

Pte C. C. Newbury,
4th Regiment.
N. Z. R.

THE PEOPLE'S ESTATE

THE NATIONAL TRUST AND THE PEOPLE OF SHEFFIELD

The whole of the Longshaw Estate, comprising 11,533 acres (4,659 hectares), was sold by the Duke of Rutland in 1927. Sheffield Corporation bought 3,000 acres (1,212 hectares) of Longshaw for water-collection purposes – including the area where the lodge stands. From 1928, Longshaw was open to the public. But with rumours of possible development as a housing estate, the Sheffield Association, later the Sheffield branch of the Council for the Preservation of Rural England (CPRE), led by Ethel Haythornethwaite, launched a public appeal to buy this part of the estate. By 1931 enough funds had been raised by the general public, and the Longshaw Estate as we know it today was bought and handed over to the National Trust. A crowd gathered in front of the lodge to witness the handover of the deeds. Working parties from Sheffield such as Clarion Ramblers helped to maintain the estate and they continue to do so to this day. The close links between Longshaw and the people of Sheffield are just as vital today as they were then.

Between 1929 and 1960 the lodge was a popular guest house for the Holiday Fellowship and postcards were sent around the country, telling family and friends about the wonderful holidays which could be had at Longshaw.

In 1962 the lodge was turned into residential flats, with a rent of £200 per annum. Longshaw Lodge is still run as private accommodation today and is not open to the public.

Below The handover of Longshaw Lodge to the National Trust in 1931

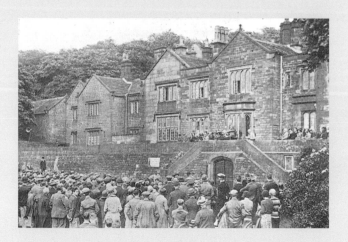

Right Longshaw Lodge as a Holiday Fellowship guest house

To Rosa Glenton in Hull:

'We had a lovely dinner at ? past 7 then a sing song till 10 o'clock and to bed. It is a beautifull [sic] place.'

To All at 64 Mortlake Road, Ilford, Essex:

'Here we are after a good journey. There is a splendid view from this place across the open moorland. Quite a jolly crowd (about 60–70) in the house.'

ENJOYING LONGSHAW

A SPECIAL PLACE FOR EVERYONE

Above White Edge Lodge can be rented as a holiday cottage

Below Pond-dipping

The Longshaw Estate is visited by thousands of people, many of whom have been returning over many years. The Visitor Centre is a focus for many, where delicious homemade cakes and lunches can be enjoyed whilst savouring the beautiful views across Longshaw Meadow to Higger Tor. Here you can also explore the National Trust shop and pick up leaflets and information about the estate.

Learning and discovery

Longshaw is a popular place for school visits. Throughout the summer months in particular, groups of young people turn Longshaw into their outdoor classroom, adding first-hand experiences to their curriculum studies.

In 2007 the Moorland Discovery Centre opened as a new lifelong learning centre for all. Throughout the year it offers learning opportunities to schools, colleges and groups from Sheffield and local communities. The centre is built to be friendly to the environment, from renewable timber and with a shingle roof. The heating of the building and water is sourced from the earth, and the walls and roof are insulated with Herdwick sheep fleece. The centre is run in partnership with the Peak District National Park Authority.

A special relationship has developed with our most local school in Grindleford. The children here have become National Trust Longshaw Guardians and visit the estate regularly throughout the year, to help with some of the conservation work and to find out more about the environment. We hope that these children will always regard Longshaw as a special place and will continue to visit in the future, introducing future generations to the delights of the Longshaw Estate.

Throughout the year, a programme of events offers a range of interesting and family-friendly ways in which to find out more about Longshaw, from guided walks to fungi forays, from Easter egg trails to Hallowe'en walks, from arts-and-crafts days to pond-dipping. Events leaflets are usually available in the Visitor Centre.

Holidays at Longshaw

You can also enjoy a holiday on the Longshaw estate, by staying at White Edge Lodge, which was once a home for one of the Duke of Rutland's gamekeepers. This National Trust holiday cottage, surrounded by spectacular moorland and with fantastic views all around is available to rent throughout the year.

Right Learning to carve stone

AN INTRODUCTORY WALK

From the Visitor Centre, cross the drive and turn left along the path by the fence.

1 Longshaw Lodge was built around 1827 as a shooting retreat for the Duke of Rutland. It is not open to the public.

Go through small gate. Turn right and go downhill through next gate

2 To the right is Longshaw Meadow, where, every first weekend in September, the Longshaw Sheepdog Trials are held. Across the meadow are the flat-topped hills of Higger Tor and Carl Wark, which is possibly a Bronze Age hillfort.

Follow the path through two gates and a corridor of rhododendron bushes to Longshaw Pond.

3 Longshaw Pond was built around the same time as the Lodge and once had a boathouse and a pier. Each year the National Trust wardens, with the help of volunteers, remove sedges to stop them from choking the open water.

Follow the path around the pond and through the wood.

4 Granby Wood was named after the Marquess of Granby, the Duke of Rutland's son. The National Trust replanted the wood with beech and Scots pine in 1990.

The path takes you past a Granby Information Barn to a road (B6521). Cross this and go through a small gate opposite.

5 To your left are Padley and Yarncliff Woods. This ancient woodland is the most important on the estate; it is one of the best examples of the old oak-birch woodland which once covered much of the Peak District.

Cross the bridge over Burbage Brook.

6 Hollowgate is the sunken track leading away from you uphill. Along this route, trains of up to 50 packhorses once carried millstones, timber, lead, wool, dairy products and salt across the Peak District.

Turn right at the bridge and follow the brook upstream.

7 Burbage Brook starts on the moorland above the estate and flows down to join the River Derwent at the bottom of the valley. Notice the alder trees on the bank sides. They need damp or wet ground to survive. The moorland area around you is called Lawrence Field.

Continue up to the next bridge and follow the path uphill.

8 Footpath work was carried out here by the National Trust wardens using an old technique known as 'stone pitching' – embedding small stones in the ground like cobblestones.

Continue uphill and take the right-hand path when you come to a junction near the stream. Continue through the wood until you come to a white gate.

9 The Duke's Gate is one of seven such gates on the estate. They were designed to be opened by a horse-rider without dismounting.

Cross the road by the entrance lodge.

10 The guidestoop behind the yew tree just inside the gate was erected in 1737, not far from where it now stands. It served as a signpost for travellers crossing the moors.

Return to the Visitor Centre along the drive.

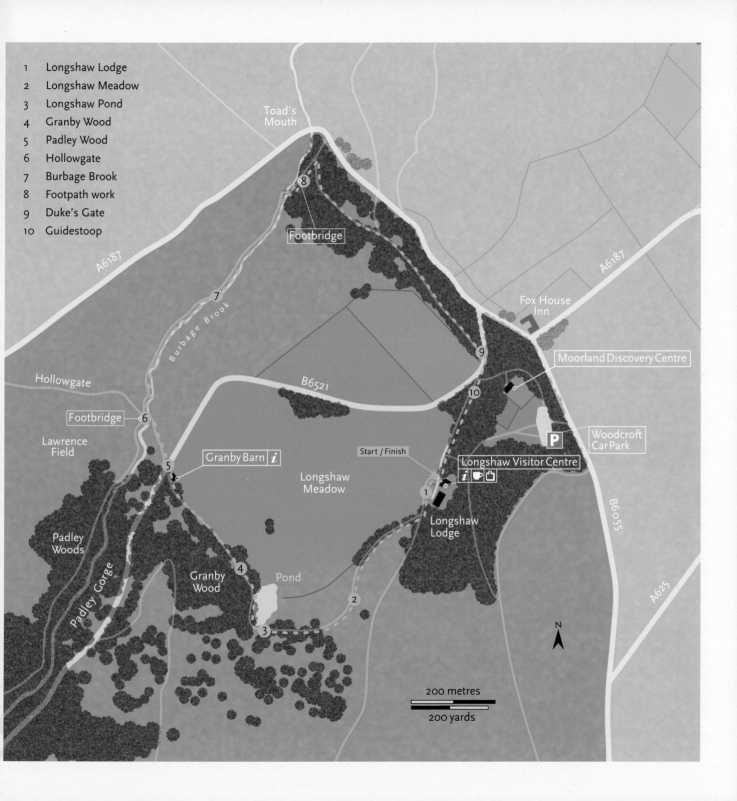

1 Longshaw Lodge
2 Longshaw Meadow
3 Longshaw Pond
4 Granby Wood
5 Padley Wood
6 Hollowgate
7 Burbage Brook
8 Footpath work
9 Duke's Gate
10 Guidestoop

Toad's Mouth

8

Footbridge

A6187

7

Burbage Brook

Hollowgate

Footbridge 6

Lawrence Field

5

Granby Barn *i*

Padley Woods

Padley Gorge

Granby Wood 4

Pond

3

Longshaw Meadow

Start / Finish

1

Longshaw Lodge

Fox House Inn

A6187

9

Moorland Discovery Centre

10

B6521

Longshaw Visitor Centre
i

P

Woodcroft Car Park

B6055

A625

N

200 metres

200 yards